MARC PICARD OFM Cap.

The Icon of the Christ of San Damiano

Casa Editrice Francescana
Frati Minori Conventuali

Nihil obstat: imprimatur
Assisi - Aprile 2000
P. Giulio Berrettoni
Custode della Basilica Patriarcale di S. Francesco

Index

In this work Marc Picard, a Canadian Capuchin priest, leads us to the marvelous discovery of an icon made for us, Westerners of the Twentieth Century.

An Icon Easy to Read

This icon is something of a caricature. The figure of Jesus, large and imposing, points him out as the "first and the last", the center of history. From the facial expressions and positions of the other characters, it is easy to guess what they are thinking. There are many characters on the icon that, by their different sizes and positions, give us the impression that we are looking at a type of cartoon, such as we might see on television.

An Icon for Little Ones

When the author presented this icon to a group of ten-year-old children, he was delighted by their reaction. They liked it very much and were able to understand it, at least partially. But the icon addresses itself to other "children" to the sinners that all are. Who does not recognize himself or herself in the figure of Mary Magdalen, in the Centurion, or in the executioners who crucified Jesus? What a joy it is to discover that all these persons resemble Jesus and Mary, and that we do too!

An Icon for Adults

Even theologians can find great pleasure in reading the immense and profound messages of this icon. In the large figure of Jesus, they can see the Primacy of Christ. His garment identifies him as High Priest of the New Covenant interceding for us in heaven. And finally, they might also see in him an image of the "Fruitful Vine" whose divine sap, flowing from the blessing hand of the Father, bears much fruit — which is to say, all those persons depicted beneath his arms.

An Icon of Hope

Here we see the Risen Jesus, victorious over death and evil. The black color in the background represents evil and emphasizes the concept of his victory. The Virgin Mary smiles at John. Jesus, shown ascending into heaven, is also smiling. All the characters are shown in a state of joy. Among them is the Centurion, along with his entire saved family, carrying his healed son on his left shoulder.

A unique Icon

This icon is very likely to spark our interest in other icons as well. It is quite sure to produce feelings of joy in us and, in these troubled times, to made us witnesses of the Resurrection.

The Christ of San Damiano

Preface

Most people of the West have the tendency to view an icon as something strange. Accostomed to seeing images that are beautiful, but only touch the emotions, they find it hard to believe that an icon can speak a most profound message, bringing one face to face with the mystery of God.

With my own Western reflexes it was quite some time before I discovered the richness of the Christ of San Damiano. Even though I am a son of St. Francis, I had very little interest in this icon until the day when I understood that it was completely inspired by St. John's Gospel. Since I had never studied Art to any special degree, I set about to uncover the secrets of the icon in the light of the Scriptures. I said to myself: "If, in creating this icon, the painter was filled with the Sacred Scriptures, then, by scrutinizing the same Holy Scriptures I will begin to understand".

A fellow Franciscan, Fr. Dominique Gagnan, a scholar in Medieval and Franciscan studies, had delved into the icon well before me. He scoured all the libraries of Europe looking for an explanation but all in vain. Some months before his unexpected death in 1980 at the age of forty, we met and exchanged our findings on the subject. It was he who showed me the meaning of the symbols we see on the icon, for example: the seashells, the circle, the rooster, etc. We were at that point when my brother, Dominique, died. I had to go on alone in the exploration, but the interest that the faithful showed for this crucifix sustained me during my research. However, these few pages on the Christ of San Damiano make no scientific pretentions. Any additions or corrections concerning this article will be welcomed.

After the biblical "reading" of the icon, readers will find some suggestions for group prayer on the major themes contained in the icon. These suggestions, or points for prayer have been added at the request of some persons who have acquired a taste for prayer together in the presence of the icon.

Presentation

The icon is called "The Christ of San Damiano" because for ages it was hung in the little church of Assisi named San Damiano. The young St. Francis was praying before this image when he heard a voice coming from the crucifix: "Francis, go, repair my house which, as you see, is falling into ruin" (2 Cel 10). Francis took these words literally and began to repair the little chapel where he prayed. Later he understood that it was the great Church of Jesus that he had to repair. At the end of his life Francis had accomplished the task he had been given; there were more than fifteen thousand Friars Minor of all nationalities. They rebuilt the Church by means of a totally new proclamation of the Gospel.

The Christ of San Damiano is a twelfth century icon, painted by a Syrian monk. It could well be titled, "The Icon of Christ in Glory". in fact, all the glory of the mystery of Christ and of his Church is depicted on this icon. It contains a surprising wealth of rich teachings. Unfortunately, those who are not familiar with the genre of iconography are slow to appreciate this type of work.

May we ask such persons to put forth a bit of effort in order that they might make the rich discovery of the sublime message of this icon. Our Western artists seek to please the eye, but their message is rather limited. An icon, instead, is created to reveal the essence of profound mystery. It does so at times, at the loss of fidelity to anatomy. For example, to express the power with which Jesus breathed forth the Spirit upon the Apostles, the iconographic painter portrays the throat of Jesus much larger than its natural proportions. Aesthetics are sacrificed for the benefit of the spiritual message.

Before entering into contemplation of the "Mystery of Christ in Glory" it would be fitting to pray to the Holy Spirit that has taught the heart and guided the hand of the author of the icon.

"Come, Spirit of Light, enlighten our hearts and enable us to appreciate the profound teaching contained in this icon. Bring about in us the mysterious transformation of ourselves into the object of our love, according to the words of St. John: "We shall be like him for we shall see him as he really is" (1 Jn 3,2)... because "to contemplate is to become". And we pray that the whole Church might once again fulfill that prophecy of Amos (Am 9,11) reiterated in the Acts of the Apostles (15,16): "After these things I will come back and I will rebuild the tottering hut of David".

A Johannine Icon

Right from the beginning it is important to note that this icon is definitely based on the Gospel of John. The crown of glory that replaces the usual crown of thorns is an evident sign of this fact. Suffering and death are transformed into glory. The prayer of Jesus is now answered: "Father, glorify your Son" (Jn 17,1). The characters shown beneath the arms of Jesus have all been presented to us by St. John. The wound in Jesus' right side is also one of the testimonies made by the Beloved Disciple.

The synoptic gospels of Matthew, Mark and Luke, reveal to us the human aspects of the life of Jesus, much like our Western images. By contrast, this icon speaks to us of the profound mystery of Christ, Word of God, in the style of St. John.

The Fourth Gospel describes the struggle between light and darkness (Jn 1,5). The final outcome of this battle shines out in this icon. The victorious body of Christ appears all the more luminous against the dark background; the black color being symbolic of opposition to the light, of unbelief, of sin. Meanwhile, the color red, symbolic of love, found all about the icon, dramatizes the victory of Light and Love over darkness.

The frame

The border of the icon sets the tone immediately. It is formed of a great number of shells. Among the ancients, the seashell had become a symbol of the beauty and eternity of heaven because of its beauty and endurance. So this border of seashells shows us that the icon is destined by its very nature to reveal heavenly mystery. However, the border is not fully complete. It is not closed at the base but a space has been left free to allow for an entry. Right at the opening we see some characters who might be recognized as believers. Two are easily discernible; the others have probably been erased by the kisses of the faithful venerating the icon throughout the ages. One sees only the upper part of their bodies. In the superior part of their being, then, in their souls, they are already living in heaven, in the Kingdom, in the new earthly paradise.

Jesus, by his large size in the center of the icon, appears as the Tree of Life in the Holy City (Gn 2,9; Rv 22,14.19). The characters beneath his arms "in the light of the Lord" (Rv 22,5) are the living fruit: "If the grain of wheat dies, it bears much fruit" (Jn 12,24).

Thus this icon reveals to us the Kingdom of God. We are already there by the faith which gives us entry; at the same time we are not yet capable of clearly discerning spiritual realities: "We see as in a mirror, dimly" (1Co 13,12).

Finally, the base of the icon seems to be formed of a block of stone. Logically, this reminds us of the Rock, that is, the authority of Peter, which is the visible seat of the Kingdom according to the words of Jesus: "You are Peter and upon this rock I will build my Church" (Mt 16,18).

The Crown of glory

Together with the border, the crown of glory around the head of Jesus, makes us understand the whole icon. The sorrowful mystery of Christ is neither forgotten nor hidden. Instead it discovers its meaning and fulfillment in glory. We must remember this when we attempt to identify the feelings of the other characters on the painting. Jesus is already glorified. Therefore, it is only proper that those around him should also be in a state of joy. We have to read the entire icon in the light of this crown[1].

In Jesus' crown of glory we see the outline of the cross, but now this cross is bathed in light. The crown, with the cross within it, summarizes Jesus' life; his humiliation and his exaltation. St. Paul says: "Though by nature he was divine, he humbled himself even unto death on a cross. For this reason God has exalted him... so that every

---

[1] We say "read" an icon, not look at an icon, because each particular detail of an icon is, in itself, something to understand and not only a thing to look at, as in any common picture. Therefore, I look at a picture and I read an icon.

tongue proclaim that Jesus Christ is the Lord, to the glory of God the Father" (Ph 2,6-11).

How this crown is full of consolation! It gives meaning to every suffering. It reminds us that every crown of thorns can be changed into a crown of glory. It proclaims the victory of life through death. Jesus said: "If the grain of wheat dies, it bears a rich harvest" (Jn 12,24).

Lord, Holy Spirit, increase our faith and make us glorious witnesses of the Resurrection of Jesus, in a world that is sad and without hope.

The Vestment of Jesus

It is very important to take note of the vestment that Jesus is wearing since by this vestment we will know what office he is exercising in this icon. From all the evidence it appears to be a loincloth of linen with a gold border. The linen and gold were used for priestly vestments (Ex 28,42). The size of the loincloth was usually quite small. One of the prescriptions of the liturgy specified that the priest should not ascend the steps to the altar for fear of immodesty (Ex 20,26). It is a simple loincloth, Egyptian style, which in Hebrew is known as the ephod (cf. 1S 2,18).

Another passage of the Bible confirms the use of this small garment by the priests. We read of David exercising his priestly function. In Mt 12,4 Jesus recognized that David acted as priest.

"David sacrificed an ox and a fat sheep; David danced, wheeling round with all his strength before Yahweh, and wearing a linen loincloth... He and all the people cried out in acclamation with the sound of the horn. David offers holocausts and communion sacrifices... He blesses the people and makes a distribution of a roll and a portion of dates. It is then that his spouse, Michal, reproaches him for having displayed himself as a commoner (2S 6,13-20). This remark by Michal leads us to understand that David's vestment was truly short. So there is no doubt: Jesus is wearing a similar loincloth and is acting here as a priest.

With David as our point of comparison, we contemplate Jesus who fulfills to perfection the priesthood of the New Covenant. David immolates animals and offers holocausts. Jesus will say: "You did not want sacrifice or oblation but a body you have prepared for me" (Heb 10,5-7). Jesus substitutes himself for the animals; he is the Lamb, he himself is the victim, and this since his birth.

Dancing and whirling about with all his might before the Lord, David prophesied the unspeakable ardor that was to burn in the heart of Jesus the priest. With inverse logic we can compare the corporal expression of David's priestly zeal with the pierced hands and feet of Jesus. The fact that Jesus was nailed hands and feet reminds us by contrast of the joyous dance of David.

While David cried out acclaimations at the sound of the horn, Jesus on the cross cried out, "I thirst", by which he meant to say: "I love you my God; I love you my people, my spouse!" This was the cry of him who is the Bridge, the link between heaven and earth. And now, in his glory, the Lamb proclaims: "Great and wonderful are your works, O Lord, God Almighty; just and true are all your ways, O King of the Nations" (Rv 15,3).

David blessed the people. Jesus, dying, pours out the Spirit (Jn 19,30) which is the blessing par excellence, eternal life.

David distributed a roll, a portion of dates and raisins; the abundance and the sweetness of this food accompanied the sacrifices, announced the Eucharist in which Jesus gives himself as food for eternal life.

Finally, David went to bless his house. He added a special benediction for his own family. In the New Covenant, to be related to Jesus no longer depends upon human kinship, but it is the fruit of fidelity to his Word. "My mother and my brothers are those who hear the Word and put it into practice" (Lk 8,21). Thus, the extent of Jesus' blessing will be the extent of our fidelity to his Word.

Blessed be you, O Father, for the burning love and generosity of Jesus, our High Priest. May the life-giving Spirit come to us! Make us become, in him and through him, a pleasing offering to you.

Jesus Temple of the Trinity

At the center of the breast of Jesus we can discern the faint outline of the head of a person. It is almost in profile and turned toward

Jesus' left side. It represents the Father of whom Jesus says, "... as you, Father, are in me..." (Jn 17,21).

Beneath this figure of the Father, there is a circle. For the ancients, the circle was a symbol of eternity because it has no beginning and no end. In the circle we can see, in profile and again, facing the left side of Jesus, the head of another person. The fact that he is within the circle tells us that the person is eternal. It represents the Word of God, eternal in his divine nature, pre-existing, Jesus of Nazareth. Lastly, on the forehead of Jesus, one can see a dove as if descending, with outspread wings. It is the Holy Spirit. Thus the words of St. Paul are recalled: "In Christ the fullness of divinity resides in bodily form" (Col 2,9). The comment given by the Jerusalem bible adds: The Risen Christ, through his resurrection, united the divine and the created. The former is what he is by his pre-existence. Therefore the body of Jesus is this living temple of which he was able to say: "Destroy this temple and in three days I will raise it up" (Jn 2,19).

By the Holy Spirit we have become living stones of this temple (1P 2,5). We adore the Trinity that lives within us. Such is our divine vocation: to be inhabited by the Trinity and to live within the three Divine Persons. As Jesus said, "Father, may they be one in us as you are in me, and I in you. So that the world may believe that it was you who sent me" (Jn 17,21). So then, the indwelling Trinity ought to mark our lives in such a way that we might become irrefutable witnesses, proclaiming that Jesus was truly sent by the Father.

The Veil over the Face of Jesus

If one looks carefully at the icon it becomes evident that both the face of Jesus and the Crown of Glory are slightly veiled. Their brilliance is muted by a shadow that extends as far as Jesus' neck. As the glory of the Lord was formerly veiled by a cloud (Ex 24,16), now this glory is veiled by the humanity of Jesus. St. Paul calls this veil, the flesh of Jesus (Heb 10,20). At the time of the Transfiguration, the veil was lifted in a certain manner and the glory of Jesus was manifest.

"His face shone like the sun and his clothes became as white as

the light" (Mt 17,2). Only Peter, James and John saw his glory. The Gospel of St. John, extends this rare privilege to all believers in a very realistic way. In fact, for John, the true believer is already in the presence of the glory of Jesus. Thus Jesus will say to Martha: "If you believe, you will see the glory of God" (Jn 11,40). At the wedding of Cana, John says: "He showed his glory and his disciples believed in him" (Jn 2,11). Take note that the cousins of Jesus were also at the wedding, but they did not believe (Jn 7,5) and they did not see his glory for the reason that since they were his close relatives, they considered only his humanity.

St. Paul also emphasizes the futility of knowing Jesus only according to the flesh: "Even if we did once know Christ in the flesh, that is not how we know him now" (2Co 5,16). Be glad! The shadow that veils the glory of Christ can be partially dissipated even in this world. Yes, to the extent that we faithfully look at Jesus, not in a human way, but in a spiritual way. To that same extent we will see his glory. "It is the spirit that gives life; the flesh has nothing to offer" (Jn 6,63).

The Eyes of Jesus

The eyes of Jesus, opened wide, show him to be the Living one, par excellence. He himself says: "Do not be afraid... I am the First and the Last, the Living One. I was dead but now I live forever and ever" (Rv 1,17-18). He is the Prince of Life (Ac 3,15) and Life itself (Jn 14,6). Besides, he wishes to bring us into that same life, "since he is living forever to intercede for all who come to God through him" (Heb 7,25).

The eyes of Jesus are very large, disproportionately so. This is a way of saying that he is the "Seeing One", the only one who sees the Father (Jn 6,46), because he is "always turned towards him" (Jn 1,18). Jesus wants to share with us his vision of the Father, revealing him to us and exorting us to see the Father in himself: "Who sees me, sees the Father" (Jn 14,9). And St. John makes it even clearer: "All we know is, that when it (the future) is revealed we shall be like him because we shall see him as he really is" (1 Jn 3,2).

Here we might ask the question, "Why are the eyes of Jesus focused between heaven and earth? As we have seen, in this icon Jesus is High Priest offering himself to the Father for all mankind. Being mediator (Heb 8,6), his glance is directed half way between heaven and earth. His glance is grave and serene at the same time. It is grave because Jesus is perfectly aware of how important is the drama of which he is central; it is serene because he knows that "the gates of hell will not prevail against his Church" (Mt 16,18).

Another good thing for us to know is that the eyes of Jesus also see us. He is the shepherd with the penetrating vision, who "knows his sheep and calls each by name" (Jn 10,3.14).

Let us not waste any time then; let's begin now to contemplate the Father in his Image, Jesus (Col 1,15). Let us become "seers" in the "Seeing One".

The Neck of Jesus

Notice how large and strong looking is the neck of Jesus. It is that way in most icons, even those that represent Jesus as a child.

The reason is this, that after the Resurrection, Jesus appeared to his disciples, breathed on them and said: "Receive the Holy Spirit. For those whose sins you forgive, they are forgiven" (Jn 20,22). The Greek word for breath recalls the moment of the creation of man (Gn 2,7) and suggests that the breath of Jesus brings about a new creation, a true resurrection (Ezk 37,9; Rm 4,17).

Pause for a moment. Let us imagine sin as a deadly gangrene plaging all men, and in fact, devouring most of them for ages and ages. To heal this gangrene, to restore humanity and to make of it a new creation, Jesus breathes his spirit upon the Apostles. Now we can imagine with how much force Jesus breathes his spirit and now we can understand why the icon portrays Jesus with such an enlarged neck. (Learn from this example of the neck of Jesus, to appreciate the powerful teaching of an icon).

Lord Jesus, thank you for having left to your Church this power of re-creation. Thank you for the Sacrament of Forgiveness in which we are healed. Grant us the grace to approach this sacrament with faith and thanksgiving. Keep us from forgetting that at the cost of your Passion and Death, you merited for us the Spirit of Life. "He was speaking of the Spirit which those who believed in him were to receive; for there was no Spirit as yet because Jesus had not yet been glorified" (Jn 7,39).

The Wounds of Jesus

The wounds in the hands, feet and side of Jesus have become fountains that are flowing abundantly with the Blood of the Lamb of God. It is the blood of the New Covenant "that has won for us an eternal redemption. Christ, having offered himself as a victim without blemish, will purify our inner self from dead works so that we

might serve the Living God" (Heb 9,12-14).

Two angels gaze intently at the wounds in Jesus' hands. Other angels under the arms of Jesus express their astonishment before the spectacle of the blood shed by the Only Son of God.

St. Peter writes, "Even the angels long to catch a glimpse of these things" (1 P 1,12), the sufferings of Christ and the glories that would come after them.

Contemplate with thanksgiving the wounds of Jesus that have become fountains of life. "By his wounds we have been healed" (Is 53,5). Let us pause before the wound in the right side of Jesus. According to the specialists who have studied the Holy Shroud, it would have been necessary for the lance to have pierced the right side in order for the blood and water to have flowed from there. The prophet Ezechiel (47,2) in speaking of the temple, said twice that a stream flowed from the right side of the temple. This temple was a symbol of the Body of Christ which is the site of the new spiritual worship. The water that flows like a torrent from the temple invigorates everything along its path and gives the trees an extraordinary fruitfulness. "Their fruit will serve as food and their leaves as medicine" (Ezk 47,12). Such is the efficacy of the living water that springs from the right side of Christ. As to the blood of Jesus, it has been poured out for our redemption and purification, as St. Paul explains: "Christ has entered the sanctuary once and for all, taking with him not the blood of goats and bull calves, but his own blood, having won an eternal redemption for us. The blood of goats and bulls and the ashes of a heifer are sprinkled on those who have incurred defilement, and they restore the holiness of their outward lives. How much more effectively the blood of Christ, who offered himself as the perfect sacrifice to God through the eternal Spirit, can purify our inner self from dead actions so that we do our service to the living God" (Heb 9,11-14).

The Characters under the Arms of Jesus

The painter of the icon has taken upon himself to identify the characters placed beneath the arms of Jesus. We can read their names written at their feet. From left to right they are: Mary, John,

Mary Magdalen, Mary the Mother of James, and the Centurion.

Since they are placed so close to Jesus we can affirm that his ardent prayer has been granted: "Father, I want those you have given me to be with me where I am, so that they may always see the glory you have given me" (Jn 17,24). These figures, moreover, are all bathed in the light. They have become "children of the Light" (Jn 12,36). Of them it is written, "The Lord God will be shining on them. They will reign forever and ever" (Rv 22,5). It is also noteworthy that all the characters are exactly the same size. This detail means that the most important thing is not the personal holiness of each one, but that Christ is "all in all" (Col 3,11). For them the words of St. Paul have already come to pass: "We are all to come to unity in our faith and in our knowledge of the son of God until we become the perfect man fully mature, with the fullness of Christ himself" (Ep 4,13).

Lastly, it is very helpful for us to discover that the characters resemble one another, all having the same large eyes, small mouths, and oval shaped faces. If we look at Jesus we find the same characteristics. The words of St. Paul suddenly come to our hearts: "They are the ones he chose specially, long ago, and intended them to become true images of his Son" (Rm 8,29). And this Son is "the living image of the Father" (Col 1,15). Also, "He who has seen me has seen the Father" (Jn 14,9). Thus in him we have been fashioned in the same image of the Father. In Jesus, the original design of God is restored: "Let us make man in our own image, in the image of ourselves" (Gn 1,26).

Mary

On the icon, Mary is at the extreme right of Jesus. In the East, this is the place of honor. The psalmist says, "At your right hand is the Queen in gold of Ophir" (Ps 45,10). Mary is "she who has found grace with God" (Lk 1,30). She is the New Eve, the mother of the Incarnate Word, and our mother according to the Spirit. Her face, turned towards John, radiates with a tenderness full of admiration. She hears always the words of Jesus: "Woman, behold your son" (Jn 19,26). She sees Jesus in John and contemplates the mystery of the

LON
GI
NU
SCA
MARIA
S IOANNES

living Christ in his members. "I am the Vine and you are the branches" (Jn 15,5).

Mary expresses her admiration before this mystery of Jesus living in John, by putting her left hand to her face. Her gesture, and that of Mary Magdalen, is done in outline so as not to hide their faces. In the Bible this gesture is well known (cf. Ws, 8,12; Jb 21,5; 29,9). She looks upon John with a gaze of indescribable tenderness and smiles gently. Since we are "the rest of her children" (Rv 12,17), her glance extends even to us. If we do all that Jesus tells us (Jn 2,5), her smile will also shine upon us. The smile of Mary reminds us of the joyful announcement of the angel Gabriel: "Be joyful, Mary" (Lk 1,28). This smile confirms that her prophecy is fulfilled: "All generations will call me blessed" (Lk 1,48). She and Jesus are the only two that are smiling in this icon.

Mary's right hand is pointed towards Jesus. This gesture signifies that he is not only the object of her conversation with John, but also that he is the fullness of both their lives. Once, by a similar gesture at Cana, she led the servants to discover in Jesus, the Spouse of the New Covenant, saying to them, "Do whatever he tells you" (Jn 2,5).

As to the beauty of Mary's face, it is the exact reflection of that of Jesus. All the women of the Old Testament who were precursors of Mary, had outstanding beauty. Remember Sara, the mother of Isaac (Gn 12,14); Rebecca, Isaac's wife (Gn 24,16); Rachel, mother of Joseph (Gn 26,7); Judith, the heroine (Jdt 8,7); and Esther, the queen (Est 1,11).

Mary's Garments

In the Bible, clothing generally reveals the true nature of the person (Rv 3,4; Is 52,1; 61,3; Lk 7,25). And so the icon uses the symbolic language of clothing to demonstrate the divine vocation of the person.

First of all, we see that Mary is clothed in a great mantle of white. It covers her completely. This white mantle carriers a three-fold message. In the first place it expresses the victory of fidelity to the Gospel: "The victor shall be clothed in white" (Rv 3,5). How well this white mantle is suited to her who has crushed the head of the serpent (Gn 3,15). Secondly, white vestments are a sign of the purification wrought by Christ (Rv 7,14). Justly Mary can be so clothed, she who from the beginning was preserved from every stain. Lastly, this vesture is a sign of the good works that God gives to the saints to accomplish, "Behold the wedding of the Lamb, His bride is ready, and she has been able to dress herself in dazzling white linen, because her linen is made of the good deeds of the saints" (Rv 19,7). If we remember that "this is the work of God, to believe in him" (Jn 6,29) we must conclude that Mary is most worthy of this mantle, she "who believed in the Word" (Lk 1,45) to the point of carrying him in her womb; she, who introduced the faith to his disciples at Cana; she, who gave birth to Life, for our sake on Calvary.

On the white mantle are seen a great number of precious stones arranged in rows. The jewels and precious stones symbolize the gifts of the Holy Spirit (see Gn 24,22; Ezk 28,13; Is 61,10). Mary is entirely covered with them. The jewels represent the divine favor with which Mary was and continues to be covered, according to the greeting of Gabriel (Lk 1,28): "Rejoice, O Full of Grace!" This title, "Full of Grace", is the name of Mary before the Lord; the name which expresses her profound reality in the eyes of God. So the precious stones tell us the divine name of Mary: she who is full of divine favor, or full of grace.

Under the great mantle, Mary wears a dark red vestment. Since red is the symbolic color of love, dark red signifies intense love; love made deeper by her particular strength. How well this color is suited to the woman who has carried in her heart all her life, the dagger of pain, and who, in the most cruel suffering at the foot of the cross, became our mother: "Woman, this is your son" (Jn 19,26).

Finally we see that Mary is wearing a violet tunic. Violet reminds us that she is the Ark of the Covenant which contained the Word of God made flesh, Jesus Christ. In fact, the interior of the ancient Ark of the Covenant was lined with purple cloth (Ex 26,1-4), and contained the two stone tablets on which were engraved the ten commandments spoken by Yahweh (Dt 10,1-5). This ark was the figure of the Virgin who was going to carry in her womb, the living Word, Jesus Christ. Mary, true Ark of the Covenant, help us to welcome the Word with a simple heart and to put it into practice (Lk 8,21).

John

In the icon, John, the beloved disciple, is nearest to Jesus as he was at the Last Supper (Jn 13,23). He truly holds the place par excellence of love, between Jesus and Mary, under the wound of love from which springs water and blood. John represents us, the believers.

John's head is turned and inclined towards Mary, his mother according to the Spirit. He has the attitude of a child that knows himself to be loved, and that welcomes that love. His right hand, like that of Mary, points to Jesus, the object of their tenderness and adoration.

John's mantle is rose colored. Traditionally, this color symbolizes love of eternal wisdom. In the Wisdom books of the Bible, one finds this: "She (wisdom) lets herself be found by those who seek her" (Ws 6,13). The first words that Jesus had spoken to John were these: "What do you want?... and (John) stayed with him the rest of that day" (Jn 1,38). John is, then, the one who has preeminently found Jesus, Wisdom itself. The affection that he received from Jesus is expressed by this phrase from the same wisdom: "I love those who love me; those who seek me eagerly, shall find me" (Pr 8,17).

John's white tunic signifies his victory over the flesh, the perfect chastity which tradition attributes to him. This chastity had merited him to receive wisdom, "which does not live in a body ladened with sin" (Ws 1,4) and to receive the Holy Spirit in abundance.

Mary Magdalen

Closest to Jesus on the left, we find Mary Magdalen. Thus the words of Jesus are fulfilled: "Some who are last will be first, and some who are first now will be last" (Lk 13,30). In her clothing bright red predominates, the symbol of love. This color is appropriate for the woman of whom Jesus said: "She has loved much" (Lk 7,47). Note that Mary Magdalen's head touches that of Mary, the mother of James. This detail leads us to understand that they are not simply conversing, but that they are sharing a secret. Considering that Mary Magdalen is putting her left hand to her mouth, like Mary, the mother of Jesus we can deduce that similarly, she is in a state of wonder and astonishment. The cause of this awe would be the incredible secret that she reveals to her companion: "On earth I was a prostitute and now, look at me standing close to Jesus".

It appears evident that on this icon, Mary Magdalen, of whom seven demons had gone out (Lk 8,2) is identified as the prostitute of Luke 7,37, of whom Jesus says: "She has loved much" (Lk 7,47). This opinion conforms with the secular tradition in the West. In fact, there was in the West a long and strong spiritual tradition identifying Mary Magdalen as the sinner in Luke 7,37. Note that immediately after the episode of the sinful woman, Luke presents Mary Magdalen to us as the woman freed from seven demons (Lk 8,2).

How the power and the love of Jesus shine forth in this woman, at one time possessed by a multitude of evil spirits (Lk 8,2), and now placed nearest to him in his glory! She had accompanied him in his journeys and then even as far as Calvary (Lk 8,2; Jn 19,25). She was the messenger sent to the Apostles to tell them: "I have seen the Lord!" (Jn 20,18). Without a doubt Mary Magdalen was with Mary and the other women in the Cenacle (Ac 1,14). With what great fervor she must have invoked the Holy Spirit, having known the horror of being possessed by many evil spirits (Lk 8,2)!

Mary, the Mother of James

According to Matthew's Gospel (27,56; 13,55) this Mary would be the mother of James, a cousin of Jesus. She is mentioned as being with Mary at the foot of the cross. Undoubtedly we would be able to find her among those women who customarily accompanied the Apostles, and who were "assiduously at prayer" (Ac 1,14), preparing themselves in this way to be baptized with the Holy Spirit (Ac 1,5).

Despite her relationship 'in the flesh' which inhibited many of Jesus' relatives from believing in him (Jn 7,5), Mary, the mother of James remained faithful to him all the way to Calvary. Does she not, perhaps, represent the multitude of humble and forgotten believers of history that one day the judgement of God is going to crown with glory?

The earthen color of her garment is a sign of her humility. The light green of her robe shows us a symbol of the firm hope that must have dwelt in her heart, even when she was at the foot of the cross. She listens attentively to what Mary Magdalen is confiding to her. The gesture of their hands suggests boundless admiration for Jesus who has redeemed his friend from the snares of the demon and from the chains of sin.

The Centurion

It is with certitude that we can identify the centurion as the royal officer of whom Jesus cured his son at a distance. (Jn 4,46) In fact, it is said of this man that he believed; he and his entire family (Jn 4,53). On his left shoulder we can see his son's face and if we look attentively behind the boy there are the foreheads of three persons. These three persons represent the centurion's family who had all been brought to the faith. The painter did not place a halo around the centurion's head, probably in order to save space for the placement of his son. However, the faith of this man is expressed in two ways. First of all, his eyes fixed intently on Jesus manifests faith in him, and then, the three extended fingers of his right hand symbolize his belief in the Trinity, while the two fingers that remain closed show his adherence to the two natures of Christ. The centurion represents the multitude of people who have grown up without knowing God and his Son, Jesus, but who have been faithful to the constant inspirations of the Holy Spirit in their hearts.

Note that the trial he went through, that is, the illness of his son was for him the means of entering definitively into Life, he and his entire family. We see that he holds in his hand a piece of wood that recalls the synagogue that would have been built at Capernaum as reported in Luke 7,5. Shortly before the healing of the son of the centurion, St. Luke quotes Jesus' words: "Every man who listens to my words and puts them into practice, is like the one who built his house upon the rock". Since Luke has left us "an ordered account" (1,3), the centurion would be portrayed as the one who listened to the word of Jesus and then effectively puts them into practice by generosity. St. John, referring to the same healing, terminates the account saying: "He and his whole house believed" (Jn 4,53). Thus the house built on rock by the one who puts the words of Jesus into practice, would represent the house, that is, the family of one who truly believed.

The Minor Characters

In front of Mary and the Centurion we see two small, unidentified characters. Since the one on the left is wearing a uniform similar to that of the centurion, we might conclude that he too is a Roman. The character on the right is in the same position as his companion on the left: his knee raised, his hand on his hip and his eyes directed towards Jesus. Having the same posture, signified that the two are playing the same role. However the one on the right is not a Roman. These two men represent those who were charged with the execution of Jesus, the Romans and the Jews as it is written: "Judas... brought the whole cohort (Romans) to this place together with a detachment of guards (Jews) sent by the chief

LON
GI
NU
MA
VRIV

priests" (Jn 18,3). The two men illustrate that the responsibility for Jesus' death rests equally with the pagans and the Jews. We might ask why their diminutive size. That simply signifies that their role is a minor one. In the eyes of men, it appears that they have killed Jesus, whereas, in reality, "no one takes his life; he lays it down of his own free will" (Jn 10,18). These people were set against Jesus, to beat and crucify and kill him, but they succeeded only in glorifying him. We must not forget this if we ourselves should encounter persecution in our own lives.

But look at the miracle! Those same persons who crucified Jesus now have their eyes fixed on him, as it is written: "They will look on the one whom they have pierced" (Jn 19,37). In killing him, they discover that Jesus is the Son of God; their eyes are opened and they arrive at faith and life. How great is the victory of love!

The Rooster

Near the left leg of Jesus, the artist has painted a rooster. It would be anachronistic to view it as the Cock of St. Peter because the icon shows Christ glorified with his chosen ones; the time of denials is past.

In ancient times, when all was so close to nature, the rooster had become the symbol of the rising sun. This sun is Jesus, the sun which rises on the world. In fact St. Peter said: "Hold fast to prophecy until the dawn comes and the morning star rises in your heart" (2P 1,19). The prophet Balaam had already designated Jesus as the star that springs from Jacob (Nb 24,17). Isaiah adds: "I will make you the light of the nations, so that my salvation may reach to the ends of the earth" (49,6). Malachy will clarify: "But for you who fear my name, the sun of righteousness will shine out with healing in its rays" (3,20). In the Book of Wisdom the sinner says: "The light of justice has not shone for us" (5,6).

The New Testament will use the same symbolism. Zachary sings out: "God from on high will bring the rising sun to visit us" (Lk 1,78). St. John will write: "The night is over, and the real light is shining already" (1Jn 2,8).

In summation, the rooster announces that Jesus is the true light that now and forever rises upon the world. Clouds may obscure this Sun, but they are only clouds. We walk in his light in order not to stumble on the numerous obstacles in the way (Jn 11,10). Moreover, with him, we ought to be the light of the world, "so that men might see our good works and give praise to the Father in heaven" (Mt 5,16).

Characters at the Foot of the Cross

We can discern only two of the persons at the foot of the cross, probably the others have been erased, victims of the signs of devotion of the many faithful that would have kissed the base of the icon.

Who are these persons? First of all, notice that they are within the enclosure formed by the seashells, therefore they are to be considered in the kingdom. Besides this, each one has a halo, though they are not in a position to see Jesus. And finally, they are in the kingdom, but only in an incomplete way, as they are shown with only the upper part of their bodies. If we consider them carefully, we note that they respond to St. Paul's description of the Christian as a pilgrim on this earth. "Before the world was made, he chose us... to be holy (their halos) and spotless, and to live through love in his presence" (they are near Jesus) (Ep 1,4). From their position on the icon they can see Jesus, but only in an imperfect manner, "as a dim reflection in a mirror", but in a short time we shall see him face to face" (1Co 13,12). Therefore, we as Christians can recognize ourselves in these persons. Already marked by the seal of the Holy Spirit (Ep 1,13), called to his kingdom and to his glory (2 Th 2,13), but still in exile because "we retain our earthly dwelling place" (2Co

5,1-6). Besides, "though this outer man of ours may be falling into decay, the inner man is renewed every day... the troubles... train us for carrying the weight of eternal glory" (2Co 4,16). Such is the teaching of the icon.

The Rock

At the very base of the icon there appears to be a stone or a rock. Perhaps this rock represents the authority of the Pope. In fact, Jesus said, "You are Peter and on this rock I will build my Church. And the gates of Hell shall not prevail against it. I will give you the keys of the kingdom of Heaven. Whatever you bind on earth shall be considered bound in Heaven" (Mt 16,18). If we remember that the whole icon represents the kingdom and that the characters seem to issue from this surface that appears to be rock, it is logical to think of it as that rock established as the foundation of Christ, that is, the authority of Peter and his successors.

Understood well, the rock can be the carrier of a personal message for each of us; a message that is the echo of the words of Jesus: "Everyone who comes to me and listens to my words and acts on them, I will show you that he is like. He is like the man who, when he built his house, dug deep and laid the foundations on the rock" (Lk 6,47). So, the practice of the Word becomes rock. Is our spiritual edifice solid? If we put into practice the words of Jesus, yes. If not, we are heading for inevitable disaster. It is for us to decide while there is still time.

The Inscription

Above the crown of glory there is the well known writing, the first three letters of the name, Jesus in Greek: I.H.S. The complete inscription, Jesus, the Nazarean, King of the Jews is written almost entirely in full. The text summarizes the life of Jesus. His profound humiliation is affirmed by his belonging to the most despised village of Israel. "Can any good come out of Nazareth?" (Jn 1,46). His glorification is proclaimed by the universal and official declaration of his royalty.

This inscription also summarizes the judgement that men of all ages and of all places have made of Jesus. Either they view him "according to the eyes of the flesh" (2 Co 5,16), and scorn him as an impostor (Mt 27,63) or they see him according to the Spirit and receive him as the true Son of God (Mk 15,39). "It is the Spirit which gives life; the flesh has nothing to offer" (Jn 6,63). Before this inscription there is no escape; one must opt either for or against Jesus. To remain neutral is not possible. Remember the words of Jesus, "You are neither cold nor hot. I wish you were one or the other, but since you are neither, but only lukewarm, I will spew you out of my mouth" (Rv 3,15).

Jesus in the Medallion

The medallion near the top of the icon presents Jesus as living in another phase of his mystery. The ascending movement of his leg leads us to understand that it is his Ascension. He ascends towards his Father who has become also our Father, and towards his God, who has become our God. His garments of gold speak of his victory and royalty. A red scarf falls from his shoulder. This is a symbol of his dominion and kingship exercised in love (1 M 10,64).

He holds a cross in his left hand, the instrument of his victory. But the cross is now golden; it has become his royal scepter, the scepter of integrity (Ps 45,7). In fact, by this cross we will be judged,

IHS NAZARE
REX IUDEORV̄

according to St. Paul: "We preach a crucified Christ; to the Jews, an obstacle they cannot get over; to the Pagans, madness... a Christ who is the power and wisdom of God" (1Co 1,23).

If we look closely we can see that Jesus has broad smile. Now he is "anointed with the oil of gladness" (Ps 45,8). Finally his trial is over and he has come out the winner. The angels who welcome him are clothed in red and gold, just as their Lord. Those angels who had seen the Son go out from the side of the Father to go into the world, triumphantly celebrate him as he returns to the Father (Jn 16,28). What a powerful Advocate we now have, close to the Father! How can we be frightened or saddened anymore?

The Hand of the Father

In a semi-circle at the very top of the icon there appears a right hand in the gesture of blessing. It is the right hand of the Father: he whom no eye has seen, reveals himself in benediction.

However, the blessing of the Father in nothing else but the gift of the Holy Spirit, merited by the death of Jesus. That is why Jesus said, "It is good for you that I am going, because, unless I go, the Advocate will not come to you. But if I do go, I will send him to you" (Jn 16,7). In reality, it will be the Father who will send the Paraclete, the Holy Spirit, in the name of Jesus (Jn 14,26), when the latter shall have entered into his glory. Thus, the Father's blessing consists in giving the Holy Spirit.

To better understand and appreciate the benediction of the Father, we must meditate these words of Jesus: "I will pray to the Father and he will give you another Advocate who will be with you forever" (Jn 14,16). The expression, "another Advocate" means that Jesus was the first Advocate, that is, he who stood beside the sons of God to be their teacher and to provide for all their needs. The Holy Spirit will have the same role, but in an invisible manner; he is going to complete the work of Jesus (Jn 14,26), and bring us into the complete truth (Jn 16,13). The expression, "another Advocate", emphasizes that the Holy Spirit is a real person and not an impersonal power.

This then, in the magnificent reward that the Father grants to his

victorious Son: the Holy Spirit himself, as "streams of living water for all those who believe in him (Jn 7,38) for his Bride, the Church.

By his gift of "living waters", Jesus, the True Vine (Jn 15,1), will bear much fruit and will be glorified in his believers (Jn 17,1). And when the son is glorified in his believers, the Father is glorified in the son (Jn 17,1).

This Spirit, which is the Living Sap distilled from the True Vine, is also the fire of love that unites Father and Son. It is in this fire of love that the Son wishes to bring us when he cries out to the Father, "Father... may the love with which you loved me, be in them, and I in them" (Jn 17,26). And so the New Alliance is consumated in the Trinity.

Suggestions for Group Prayer before the Icon

Being an exceptional instrument for prayer, this icon will be of great profit to small communities of believers, inspiring them in their moments of prayer. They will benefit by obtaining for their use, an enlarged reproduction of the icon, or by projecting slides of the original icon on a screen.

To better appreciate the icon, one must never forget that it was through this means that Jesus entrusted St. Francis with the enormous task of rebuilding his house which was falling into ruin. How many Francis's are needed today in the church so that it might renew itself? Nor must we forget that he who at the age of twenty prayed before this crucifix became resplendent with the most abundant and magnificent gifts and graces. Two years before his death, the stigmata of Christ testified before all men that it was no longer Francis who lived, but Jesus living in him.

It might be useful to use a pointer to indicate details that are the subject of prayer which can later be shared in the group.

The person who directs the celebration should be well prepared in two ways: first, to have a good understanding of the details of the icon, and secondly, and just as important, he should pray that the Holy Spirit might himself be the soul of the prayer celebration.

For a Eucharistic Celebration

The Body of Jesus

As at Calvary and in the Mass, Jesus on the icon is being offered to the Father for all mankind. His sentiments, shown by his arms opened wide, testify that he is giving his whole being for the benefit of all humanity.

In this icon, Jesus is the Tree of Life; all those who "have washed their garments in the blood of the Lamb" can have recourse to him (Rv 22,14; 7,14) The Fruit of this Tree of Life is the Eucharist. "He who eats of this will live forever" (Jn 6,51). In contrast, those who eat from the Tree of Knowledge of Good and Evil "will certainly die" (Gn 2,17).

The Wound in the Side of Jesus

The wound in the side of Jesus shows us where this "divine folly", which is the Eucharist, has been conceived — within the heart itself of the God-Man! It is the burning fruit of his creative love. "I have longed to eat this passover with you before I suffer because I tell you, I shall not eat it again until it is fulfilled in the kingdom of God" (Lk 22,15-16). This passover, this meal together, this loving encounter of the Bridegroom and the Bride will be brought about initially in the Eucharist, and in a complete, unveiled manner at the end of time.

The Minor Characters at the Base

Be aware that we are those little people in the state of being formed. Spiritually we are like infants in our mother's womb. And our Mother, the Church, nourishes us with him who is Life itself, the Spirit of the Risen Jesus, present in the Eucharist.

For a Penitential Celebration

The Wounds of Jesus

The position of Jesus on the cross, the wounds in his hands and feet and side, tell us at what price we have been redeemed. All the pain and blood of the Only and Beloved Son were necessary in order to snatch us from the snares of sin and death.

Mary Magdalen

Mary Magdalen, the sinner, the woman with seven demons, is now placed very near to Jesus. She testifies to the power of redemption in the blood of the Lamb of God. "Even if your sins be as scarlet... they will become white as snow" (Is 1,18).

The Minor Characters

Because they have their eyes fixed on Jesus, we conclude that the Roman soldier and the Temple Guard have been brought to faith and are now saved. The power of the salvation of Jesus whom they have crucified, shines out from them. This power can shine in us too, if with the eyes of our hearts we look upon that Jesus whose word we have disregarded. If even those who have crucified Jesus have been redeemed and saved, who then can ever dispair?

Jesus in the Medallion

The icon shows us Jesus ascending victoriously into heaven, and receiving the blessing of his Father. It is he, the object of the Father's happiness (Mt 17,5), who is also "our advocate with the Father". Jesus Christ, the just one, is the victim of expiation for our sins (1Jn 2,1). In him we can trust.

The Neck of Jesus

Lastly, the enlarged neck of Jesus reminds us of the power of his breath in giving the Holy Spirit. "Whose sins you shall forgive, they are forgiven" (Jn 20,23).

For a Celebration of the Father

The Father in filigree

Look carefully at the Father, outlined almost as a watermark on Jesus' chest. Now savor the words of Jesus: "The Father and I are one" (Jn 10,30). We are filled with joy because Jesus has prayed that even we might be brought into this unity. "As you, Father, are in me, and I in you, may they be one in us" (Jn 17,21).

Now we understand how Jesus was able to say, "I am never alone, because the Father is with me" (Jn 16,32). By your presence in us, free us, Father, from lonliness; it is a sad and evil counsellor. Contemplating the Father in the Son, admire how ardent and filial was the prayer of the son. "Jesus, teach us (again) to pray".

The Hand of the Father

Now look at the Father's hand in the semicircle. Let us be reconciled to the Father who seems, at least to some people, to be cruel. It is not the Father who imposed the atrocious death upon Jesus, but it was we ourselves, sinners who did so. As far as Jesus is concerned, his love for us has always been one with that of his Father.

Savor the immense joy of the Father in blessing his Son; and not only his Son, but all those who believe in him. His blessing is eternal life, and the joy of a father is to give life.

The Son on the Cross

Since Jesus is the image of the Father (Col 1,15), we contemplate in him, the tenderness of the Father, his generous love, his strength, his simplicity, his humility. Let us approach the Father through Jesus, and let us be freed of all the painful memories we might have of our own fathers, which inhibit us from believing in the goodness of the Father towards us.

For a Celebration of the Son

The Son in filigree beneath the Father

Like the Father, the Son is invisible in his divine nature. However, because of the plan made by the Three Divine Persons, the Son accepts a mission ouside of the Trinity. He assumed a human nature and became man in order to reveal the Father and make Him visible to us. We are grateful to the Trinity for this inestimable gift.

The Body of Jesus

We see how the body of Christ covers most of the surface of the icon. It is so that, "all things subsist in him, those visible and those invisible" (Col 1,17.16). We are immersed in him as if in a creative environment. In fact, "he examines me and he knows me; he knows if I am standing or sitting; he reads my thoughts from far away" (Ps 139,2).

The Arms of Jesus

Looking at Jesus with his arms extended just as they were on the day of his sacrifice on the cross, we discover the immensity of his love for us. We discover also, the immensity of the love of the Father, whom our eyes cannot see, but whom Jesus enables us to know.

The Wounds of Jesus

In Jesus' wounds we discover the gravity of our faults and the source of our redemption. The Spirit tells us in the words of Isaiah, "He was pierced through for our faults, crushed for our sins. On him lies a punishment that brings peace; by his wounds we are healed" (Is 53,5). Since Jesus is the image of the Father we might understand the mysterious, but real suffering of the Father. We can even imagine the pain of the Holy Spirit, "who groans within us" (Rm 8,26), he whom we can sadden and even suppress (1Th 5,19). Finally, let us recall the words of St. Peter: "Rejoice, if you participate in the sufferings of Christ" (1P 4,13). It is thus that we begin to be conformed to the image of the Son (Rm 8,29).

Jesus in the Medallion

Lastly, let us carefully scrutinize the face of Jesus in the medallion. It is very young and we see that for the first time, he is smiling. Jesus is entering into the joy of the Father. He is going first, then we also, close behind him, will contemplate his glory and be united in the same love with which the Father loves; him, and the Holy Spirit.

For a Celebration of the Holy Spirit

The Dove on Jesus' Forehead

Look at the dove on the forehead of Jesus. It is his baptism that is being recalled. John the Baptist with emotions of joy said, "I saw the Spirit coming down on him from heaven, like a dove, and resting on him" (Jn 1,32). We bless the Father who, after having manifested his Son through the Incarnation, reveals the Holy Spirit to us, under the form of a dove.

We bless you, Father, for our baptism, in which you gave us the first fruits of the Holy Spirit, the seed of his gifts and charisms.

Once baptized, Jesus was led by the Spirit into the desert (Mk 1,12). Yes, the Spirit lead him far away from the easy paths, into a place of stern spiritual trianing. O Spirit of Jesus, impel us towards the adventure of the spirit. Break us away from our attachment to ease.

Thank you, Holy Spirit, for having been the power in Jesus' ministry. "The Spirit of the Lord has been given to me, for he has anointed me. He has sent me to bring the Good News to the poor, to proclaim liberty to captives, and to the blind, new sight, to set the downtrodden free, to proclaim a year of favor from the Lord" (Lk 4,18).

Spirit of Truth, create in me a poor heart so that I will be able to receive from Jesus, every healing and liberation. Make me an instrument of salvation for my brothers and sisters.

The Neck of Jesus

Spirit of Jesus, you who were breathed so powerfully upon the Apostles for the forgiveness of sins, help me to receive the Sacrament of Forgiveness with faith, efficacy, and gratitude.

The Hand of the Father

O Holy Spirit, you who were bought for us at the price of the Blood of Jesus, you who are the gift of the Father, may your power act freely in me.

For a Celebration of Mary

Mary

We bless you, Lord, for Mary, the masterpiece of your love, she whom you fashioned from our same human clay. The psalm that sings of the Royal Wedding, says of the King: "On your right stands the Queen in gold of Ophir" (Ps 45,10). It is in this way that the icon presents Mary to us, at the right side of Jesus. On her white mantle shines a transparent veil, covered with diamonds, which symbolize the gifts of the Holy Spirit.

The Face of Jesus

The same psalm continues: "Then the King will desire your beauty" (Ps 45,12). See how the face of Jesus is turned towards Mary, expressing where lies the desire of his heart. In her humility, Mary also speaks of the Lord's face turned towards her, but she will give it another meaning: "My soul glorifies the Lord, because he has turned his eyes upon the humility of his handmaid" (Lk 1,46.48). Mary, implore for us that same humility!

The White Mantle

Thank you, Mary, for your fidelity that has made you worthy to wear the white mantle of victory over all evil.

The dark red robe

Thank you, Mary, for the intense love with which you surroundend Jesus and which you unceasingly pour out upon us.

The violet Tunic

Mary, True Ark of che Covenant, you who carried the Living Word in your womb, increase in us the desire for this Word.

John

Mary, with what tenderness your eyes rest upon John. Thank you for your maternal care which always envelopes us. Heal us of all our hurts. Mary, your eyes are full of wonder because in looking at John, you see Jesus. "Woman, here is your son". Thank the Father for us because he has destined us to be members of Jesus, sons in the Son.

Right Hand of Mary

Mary, your right hand points to Jesus because he is the "All" of your heart. Beg the Holy Spirit to reveal him to us until we also are captivated by him. Mary, when you made a similar gesture at Cana, you said to the servants, "Do whatever he tells you". Pray to the Holy Spirit that we might become docile to the word of Jesus; that our lives might be overflowing with the humble efforts of everyday, as were the stone water jars at Cana.

The Wound in the Side

Mary, you were there when Jesus died and when his heart was pierced with the lance and you did not doubt the Resurrection. Obtain for us the grace of faith in the face of all our trials.

Mary, you are always near to Jesus as you were on Calvary. Be always present with us in our Eucharists. Offer Jesus to the Father and offer us in him, since you are our Mother.

For a Celebration of the Lord's Love

Jesus

We honor you, Father, because you "loved the world so much that you gave your only Son in order that whoever believed in him might have eternal life" (Jn 3,16).

The Main Characters

Father, the icon shows us the saints in your glorious light. Thank you for having made us "children of the light". Preserve us from the power of darkness.

Mary

Father, the icon presents Mary at the place of honor, at the right side of Jesus. Thank you for having so exalted your humble handmaid. Thank you for having filled her with the Holy Spirit, and for having given her to us as our Mother.

John

Father, in this icon the Apostle, John, stands between Jesus and Mary. What a privilege! What a delightful place! Let us believe that it is this very same place that has been destined for us, between Jesus and Mary, beneath the inexhaustible fountain of the heart of your Beloved.

Blessed are you, Father, for having given us John, this burning witness of the Word of Life (1Jn 1,2), of your love (1Jn 4,8), and of your Holy Spirit (Jn 19,35).

Mary Magdalen

Father, both the icon and the Gospels place John, the virgin Apostle and Mary Magdalen, the penitent, close to Jesus. We thank you for the power of the blood of Jesus that is able to unite your children who had been so far apart.

Mary, Mother of James

Blessed are you, Father, for the glory which the icon reserves for Mary, the Mother of James. This woman followed Jesus and served him (Mk 15,41). She was faithful to him until his death, and even beyond it. She was present at the Cenacle, invoking with ardent prayer, the coming of the Promised Spirit. Blessed are you, Father, for the glory you give to the humble ones. You will make them shine brightly on the Day of your Light.

The Centurion

For the heart of the pagan centurion who sought you, may you be blessed, Father. His trial, that is, the illness of his son, was for him and all his family, the pathway to Life. "Your ways are not our ways" (Is 55,8), but we wish to adore you in all your ways.

The Centuion's son

For the centurion's son, saved by the faith of his father, We bless you, Lord. Give to those parents whose children are ill, the faith to believe that their prayers touch your heart, and that one day they will be answered.

The Minor Characters

For the astonishing presence in your kingdom of the Roman soldier and the Temple guard... for those who sacrificed your only Son, we bless you, God of Mercy. Enable all those who are afflicted with sin to come to Jesus with confidence, and to find healing in his wounds (Is 53,5).

Characters at the Foot of the Cross

For all of us who are represented in these characters at Jesus' feet, we bless you. They are already crowned: "because you have chosen us to be holy and immaculate in your presence, in love" (Ep 1,4).

The Rock

Finally, does not the rock on which the icon rests represent the authority of the Pope? We thank you for the Shepherd that you have given to the Church. Grant us the docility to follow his teachings.

For a Celebration in Honor of the Angels

Before this icon where angels and men are united, we bless you, Father. You have reminded us that we are all of the same family, all created in your First-born Son, by him and for him (Col 1, 15-16), and that we are always in their holy presence.

Angels at the top

Thank you, Father, for those angels gathered together at the top of the icon. Their privileged place makes us understand that thay live intimately with you, as did our first parents in Paradise. For each of them, for their great perfection, and their burning adoration, blessed be you, O Lord.

Angels at the sides of the Cross bar

For these angels who immerse their attention in the wounds of Jesus Hands, thank you, Father. Receive in our name, their profound adoration and their limitless thanksgiving for the blood of your only Son that is being poured out for us.

The Angels beneath Jesus' arms

Thank you, Father, for these angels who are full of wonder at the discovery of the immense mystery of the Blood of Jesus. In your light they have discovered to what extent we have been loved: "To him who loves us and freed us from our sins by his own blood, who has made us a royal nation of priests in the service of his God and Father..." (Rv 1,5).

The presence of so many angels tells us that they are our intercessors and protectors. The Gospel presents them to us as real and active beings. Gabriel announces an impossible birth to Zachary and to Mary (Lk 1,11 and 26). Angels gave Jesus food to eat (Mt 4,11) and an angel consoled him (Lk 22,43). The Liturgy of the Mass recalls their presence in the Gloria, in the Preface and in the Santus. Lord, let this icon help us to come to a greater belief in the presence of the angels in our lives.